HOW TO REMOVE SPOTS AND STAINS

HOW TO REMOVE SPOTS AND STAINS

Professor Herb Barndt

Philadelphia College of Textiles and Science

A Perigee Book

Perigee Books
are published by
The Putnam Publishing Group
200 Madison Avenue
New York, NY 10016

Library of Congress Cataloging-in-Publication Data

Barndt, Herb.
How to remove spots and stains.

Includes index.
1. Spotting (Cleaning) I. Title.
TX324.B37   1987   646'.6   87-15412
ISBN 0-399-51391-4

Designed by: Anne Scatto / Levavi & Levavi

Printed in the United States of America
1   2   3   4   5   6   7   8   9   10

To my children: Stan, Mary and Mike.
Without their help I never would have known
how many stains were possible.

Get It Out! Thoughts on Stain Removal

Welcome to the world of stain removal! This book offers you the opportunity to learn what has become a lost art—removing stains from fabrics at home, instead of sending garments to the dry cleaner or throwing them out.

With the introduction of a wide array of new fabrics, the textile industry has made it harder to remove stains from our clothes. But with a little ingenuity and the techniques described here, you can remove most of the stains you'll come across. Listed below are a few tips and cautions that will help make each stain removal procedure quick, easy and profitable.

A small, inconspicuous area of the fabric—a hidden flap or cuff, for example—should always be used to test the materials and techniques described for a particular treatment to determine that no significant color loss or fabric damage will occur. Delicate fabrics, such as silk and rayon, and other fabrics of loose construction can be damaged or distorted by mechanical action, such as rubbing. Scrubbing these fabrics will usually cause a bruise mark which cannot be removed. If bleach is suggested to remove the stain, be particularly cautious about silk and wool as fabrics containing these fibers will be dissolved in chlorine bleach.

Any stain removal method has a better chance to work if you move quickly—the quicker the better. Of course, you can't rip a shirt off someone's back or pull the tablecloth from under the dinner guests' plates, but the faster you can get to a stain, the better chance there is to remove it successfully.

Upholstered furniture and floor coverings are particularly difficult to treat. In most cases, the fabric cannot be removed from the furniture and laundered or dry cleaned, and it is impractical and inconvenient to take up a carpet of any size, so the stain must be treated in place. Under these circumstances, it is almost impossible to lift all the stain and/or soil. Some residue will be dispersed into the foundation of the fabric or pile. This usually doesn't cause a problem, but the stained areas of some materials will discolor in periods of high humidity or the stains will return as gray or dark areas sometime later, for which, unfortunately, there's no easy solution.

Common sense should prevail when evaluating whether a stain can be removed in the home or whether professional help should be sought. An important consideration will be the cost and the life expectancy of the item. An expensive blouse or shirt that has been worn only a few times may demand the care available from a professional dry cleaner, whereas an older or less expensive garment is a good candidate for first experiments with these home stain removal techniques.

I hope that you'll find stain removal a simple, satisfying task—and one that will save you money. Good luck!

THE FIVE CLEANING AGENTS

In order to remove a stain, you need to apply the proper cleaning agents. The cleaning agents combine with the stain and are then removed, bringing the stain with them.

There are a number of commercial "spot removers," such as K2r, that work very well on some stains and hardly at all on others. This is because any one type of stain remover can't possibly be effective against all types of stains. There are five basic categories of cleaning agents and each works best against a particular group of stains. Combination stains (those with multiple components, e.g., sugar, fat, coloring, etc.) may require treatment with more than one cleaning agent.

Solvents

Solvents are the most important category of cleaning agents. A solvent mixes with the stain, dissolves it and forms a removable liquid or powder. Using a solvent is a three-step process. Apply the proper solvent, let it do its work and then remove it.

The major types of stain-removing solvents are:

- Oil Solvents
- Combination Solvents
- Alcohol
- Acetone
- Glycerin

Oil solvents are ideal for removing stains that contain oil or greasy substances. The solvent mixes with the stain, absorbs it and then evaporates. You don't need to remove the solvent after you apply it—though you might need to brush off the powder left behind. The oil solvent is ideal for fabrics that are sensitive to water. Remember:

- Oil solvents should *never* be used on wet fabrics, so you must always wait until the fabric has dried.
- Be sure that the room is well ventilated.
- Always test a solvent on a not normally visible portion of the fabric to be sure it won't harm the material.

K2r is the most popular stain remover on the market and contains an oil solvent and other ingredients, while Carbona Spot Remover, which is a little harder to find, contains nothing but oil solvents and may work better on some stains than K2r.

Combination solvents are a powerful alternative to oil solvents. In addition to a powerful chemical solvent, they may contain soap, glycerin or water. Combination solvents are effective against many stains, including greasy ones, and can be used on most fabrics, wet or dry.

Unlike oil solvents, combination solvents do not evaporate. After using the solvent, you must rinse it out with water. Common combination solvents include Shout, Spray 'n Wash and Magic prewash.

Note: Manufacturers often add other ingredients (like bleach) in order to enhance a solvent's performance. Unfortunately, this can occasionally wreck your clothes. Pretest carefully.

Alcohol is a very powerful solvent. Pure alcohol evaporates very quickly and can be used on fabrics that can't stand water. Rubbing alcohol, which contains water, should not be used on these fabrics. Rubbing alcohol may also contain other additives that can cause trouble.

WARNING: ALCOHOL CAN MAKE ALMOST ANY DYE RUN.

Acetone is a very specialized solvent, ideal for removing airplane glue and nail polish remover. Again, be sure to test before using.

NEVER USE ACETONE ON ACETATE OR TRIACETATE!

*ALCOHOL AND ACETONE ARE
EXTREMELY FLAMMABLE!*

Glycerin is a weak solvent but is effective as a presoak in softening some stains. It is an ingredient used in many combination solvents.

Digestants (enzyme paste)

Digestants are the most amazing of the stain removers. They contain enzymes which actually eat protein stains. Protein stains include chocolate, milk, blood, gravy, egg, etc.

To most effectively use the digestants for spot removal, you must first make a paste. Mix a spoonful or two of the digestant with an equal amount of water. Be careful not to get the paste on your skin. After testing on a corner of the fabric, apply the paste and then rinse out thoroughly.

Digestants are available in laundry presoaks like Axion or Biz. Purer formulas are available at good drugstores (ask for pepsin, papain or amylase).

*THE ENZYMES IN A DIGESTANT WILL ATTACK
WOOL AND SILK!*

Soaps

Soaps are simple yet effective stain removers. Soaps are available in two basic kinds: high-alkali, heavy-duty soaps and low-alkali unbuilt soaps. The first group includes commercial and industrial soaps. The true soaps, like Woolite, Ivory and Lux are in the second group. (Some detergents, including Tide and Cheer, are also referred to as soaps.

Soaps act as a surfactant. They join with water and stain and create a gray mess, which can then be washed off the fabric. If you place a dirty mop in a pail of soap and water, the water will soon turn a dingy color, but the mop will come out clean. This is the miracle of soap. Detergents also contain surfactants, and can be used for general-purpose washing. Pure soaps are preferred for stain removal.

Absorbents

This group of cleaning agents is the simplest in concept. An absorbent acts as a blotter to draw the stain out of the fabric. Absorbents work well only when the area is still wet from the original stain.

Common absorbents are:

- Talcum Powder
- Corn Meal
- Cornstarch

Obviously absorbents are not the most powerful cleaning agents available to you, but this is one of their best features. They almost certainly won't ruin your fabrics, and if you use them quickly enough, you will often find that they'll completely remove a spill and let you avoid using harsher methods.

Note: Be sure to test the removability of the absorbent before you use it. Removing a stain with cornstarch is no bargain if you then can't get the cornstarch out of the fabric. Be especially cautious when using absorbents on carpets and upholstery.

Bleaches

Bleaches don't actually remove a stain. Instead, they remove the color of the stain. The hierarchy of bleaches, from very strong to very mild, is:

- Chlorine
- Ammonia
- Hydrogen Peroxide
- Lemon Juice
- White Vinegar (acetic acid)
- Synthetic Bleaches (Clorox II, Snowy)

Bleaches can be diluted with water to make them weaker, and you'll get more even results if you wet the garment before applying bleach to the stained area. After using a bleach, you must thoroughly flood the area with water.

Don't discount the power of lemon juice or vinegar. A small stain on a white tablecloth can be removed before the hostess even notices! Just take some lemon off the tea tray, put a napkin under the cloth and gently apply lemon juice to the stain.

Note: Be careful not to get strong bleaches on your skin. If you do, wash with lots of water and lemon juice. And, once again, remember to test any bleach on your fabric before using it on a stain.

Following are some common substances that cause Stains. In each case, the Type of stain produced by the substance is given, as well as the cleaning agents (Formula) used to remove the stain and the Method.

Stains

STAIN

AFTER-SHAVE

TYPE

perfume, alcohol

FORMULA

glycerin
white vinegar

METHOD

Moisten the stain and add some glycerin. Rinse with water. If any stain remains, rinse with a mild vinegar-and-water solution, and rinse again with water.

STAIN

ANTIPERSPIRANT

TYPE

aluminum chloride, alcohol

FORMULA

combination solvent
liquid detergent
ammonia
bleach
oil solvent

METHOD

This is a common stain, and one that should be removed as soon as possible. The longer the stain is left untreated, the greater the chance it will set into the fabric.

If fabric is washable, pretreat stain with a combination solvent, then machine wash garment with *warm* water and liquid detergent. If colors are affected, sponge a little ammonia on the area (for wool or silk, dilute the ammonia with an equal amount of water). Be sure to rinse the garment thoroughly after using ammonia. If the garment can be bleached, do so.

If fabric is nonwashable, use an oil solvent. Spray the solvent on the stain, let dry and brush off.

STAIN

APPLE JUICE

TYPE

fruit

FORMULA

water
white vinegar
glycerin
combination solvent

METHOD

Kids are always spilling apple juice on themselves. It may not seem like a bad stain, but if not removed promptly, it can yellow the garment permanently.

Immediately sponge off the stain with *cool* water. If fabric is nonwashable, sponge stain with a solution of vinegar and water, and then plain water.

If the fabric is not fragile, spread the stained area over a bowl, and pour boiling water through the fabric from a height of 12 inches. The hot water will set the stain, but not before the force of the water washes the stain into the bowl. If the fabric can't stand boiling water, apply glycerin to stain, rinse, then treat with a combination solvent and wash garment.

NEVER USE SOAP AND NEVER IRON A FRUIT STAIN!

STAIN

APPLE PIE

TYPE

fruit, sugar, fat

FORMULA

water
white vinegar
glycerin
combination solvent
bleach

METHOD

Apple pie stains are similar to apple juice stains, with the additional problems caused by the fat in the crust.

Immediately sponge off the stain with *cool* water. If fabric is nonwashable, sponge stain with a solution of vinegar and water, and then plain water. If the fabric is not fragile, use the boiling water method: Spread the stained area over a bowl and pour boiling water through the fabric from a height of 12 inches. The hot water will set the stain, but not before the force of the water washes the stain into the bowl. If the fabric can't stand boiling water, apply glycerin to stain, rinse, then treat with a combination solvent, and wash.

After removing the apple portion of the stain, some residue from the fats may remain. Use bleach or combination solvent to remove this stain.

NEVER USE HEAT ON A SUGAR STAIN!

NEVER USE SOAP AND NEVER IRON A FRUIT STAIN!

STAIN

ASHES/SOOT

TYPE

carbon, organic materials

FORMULA

water
liquid soap
ammonia

METHOD

Fireplace ashes seem to adhere to whatever they touch. If they get into your carpet, vacuum immediately.

To remove ashes from clothes, first moisten the stain with some water. Rub in some liquid soap and then add a few drops of ammonia. If fabric is washable, rinse the stained area and machine wash the entire garment in warm soapy water. If the fabric is nonwashable, sponge the stained area with plain water to rinse.

STAIN

AVOCADO

TYPE

vegetable, oil

FORMULA

combination solvent
oil solvent

METHOD

If fabric is washable, pretreat stain with a combination solvent, then wash. For nonwashable fabrics, use an oil solvent. Spray the solvent on the stain, let dry and brush off.

This works on guacamole stains as well.

STAIN

BABY FOOD

TYPE

fruit, vegetable, protein

FORMULA

cool water
detergent or soap
bleach
white vinegar

METHOD

Fortunately, most babies don't wear clothes marked Dry Clean Only. If you can't find the specific stain listed elsewhere in this book, use the following method to be

24

sure that you don't set the stain by using the wrong procedure—many stains are set by hot water and soap, for example.

1. Sponge the stain immediately with *cool* water.
2. Soak the garment in *cool* water for up to 12 hours. This will remove most stains.
3. Rub detergent or soap into stained area, and rinse.
4. If any stain remains, use bleach. Wash garment.

If the stain is on the parent's Dry-Clean-Only garment, sponge with *cool* water and then with white vinegar.

STAIN

BABY FORMULA (SIMILAC, ETC.)

TYPE

artificial compounds

FORMULA

digestant
detergent
cool water
oil solvent

METHOD

If fabric is washable, moisten the spot with *cool* water and apply digestant paste; don't allow paste to dry out. Rinse. For nonwashable fabrics, sponge stain with detergent and *cool* water, then with plain water to rinse. Let dry and treat with an oil solvent.

===

STAIN

BABY OIL

TYPE

mineral oil, perfume

FORMULA

combination solvent
detergent
oil solvent

METHOD

For washable fabrics, pretreat stain with a combination solvent, wash garment in detergent. If any stain remains, use an oil solvent. For nonwashable fabrics, use an oil solvent. Spray the solvent on the stain, let dry and brush off.

STAIN

BACON GREASE

TYPE

animal fat

FORMULA

absorbent
combination solvent
petroleum jelly
oil solvent

METHOD

First, use an absorbent to remove as much of the grease
as possible. (This works on carpets as well.) If the fabric
is washable, apply a combination solvent and some petroleum jelly to stain and wash garment. Nonwashable
fabrics should be treated with an oil solvent.

STAIN

BAKED BEANS

TYPE

sugar, starch, tomato, grease

FORMULA

cool water
combination solvent
white vinegar

METHOD

With a dull blade, scrape off as much of the food as you can. Apply *cool* water and a combination solvent to stain. Rinse. Wash garment in *cool* water, if fabric is washable. If any stain remains, sponge with vinegar. Rinse. Wash garment again, if washable. If fabric is nonwashable, sponge stained area, first with *cool* water and combination solvent, then with plain water to rinse. Sponge with vinegar and then plain water to remove any remaining stain.

NEVER USE HEAT ON A SUGAR STAIN!

STAIN

BARBECUE LIGHTER FLUID

TYPE

petroleum distillates

FORMULA

combination solvent
oil solvent

METHOD

If fabric is washable, apply a combination solvent to stain, then machine wash garment in *cool* water. For nonwashable fabrics, try an oil solvent. Spray the solvent on the stain, let dry and brush off.

NEVER USE HEAT ON A SUGAR STAIN!

STAIN

BARBECUE SAUCE

TYPE

tomato, tannin, sugar

FORMULA

cool water
glycerin
combination solvent
white vinegar

METHOD

Rinse stain with *cool* water. Apply glycerin and a combination solvent to the stain, and rinse again.

STAIN

BEER

TYPE

water, alcohol, sugar, protein

FORMULA

cool water
white vinegar
digestant
sodium perborate or hydrogen peroxide

METHOD

Perhaps the worst part of a beer stain is the smell of flat beer. The combination of alcohol, sugar and protein requires a multi-step process for removal.

Blot up the beer with a dry cloth. Rinse the stain with *cool* water mixed with some vinegar. Rinse with plain water. Finally, apply some moist digestant paste—be sure the paste doesn't dry out or damage the fabric. Rinse again. If any stain remains, treat with sodium perborate or hydrogen peroxide. Rinse. Wash washables.

Unfortunately, there is no remedy for colors that fade or run because of the alcohol in the beer.

NEVER USE HEAT ON A SUGAR STAIN!

STAIN

BEETS

TYPE

sugar, vegetable dye

FORMULA

water
glycerin

combination solvent
digestant

METHOD

Move quickly or the stain will set. Rinse the stain with *cool* water, then apply glycerin and a combination solvent. Let sit for 5 minutes, then rinse. If any stain remains, apply digestant paste. Do not allow to dry out. Rinse.

NEVER USE HEAT ON A SUGAR STAIN!

STAIN

BIKINI WAX

TYPE

creams, oils

FORMULA

oil solvent

METHOD

Spray an oil solvent on the stain, let dry and brush off. Repeat if necessary.

STAIN

BLEACH

TYPE

dye

FORMULA

scissors

METHOD

If bleach has turned a colored fabric white, the only way to remove the spot is to cut it out. Sorry.

STAIN

BLEU CHEESE DRESSING

TYPE

oil, egg, cheese

FORMULA

absorbent
combination solvent

33

liquid soap
ammonia
oil solvent

METHOD

Salad dressings cause a difficult combination of greasy and nongreasy stains. First, using an absorbent, remove as much of the stain as you can. If fabric is washable, and the stain is still visible, treat with a combination solvent, then rinse. Apply some liquid soap to the stain, and rinse again. Finally, machine wash the garment.

If the stain is not immediately visible, apply liquid soap to stain, and wash garment. If the colors of the garment are affected, apply a mixture of 2 tablespoons ammonia to 1 cup water, and rinse with water.

If the fabric is not washable, use an oil solvent. Spray the solvent on the stain, let dry and brush off.

===

STAIN

BLOOD, DRIED

TYPE

protein, water, salts

FORMULA

cool salt water
ammonia
digestant
bleach

METHOD

Soak the garment in *cool* salt water for several hours to soften the stain. Rinse thoroughly. Soak again in water to which several tablespoons of ammonia have been added. Rinse. If any stain remains, apply digestant paste—don't let it dry out—then rinse. If the fabric can't take a digestant, try bleach, or water mixed with ammonia.

NEVER USE HEAT, NEVER USE ACIDS!

STAIN

BLOOD, FRESH

TYPE

protein, water, salts

FORMULA

cool water
ammonia
digestant

METHOD

First, stop the bleeding and save the patient! Blot up as
much of the blood from the garment as possible. Rinse
stain with *cool* water, then follow with *cool* water mixed
with a few drops of ammonia. Rinse thoroughly. If any
stain remains, apply digestant paste; don't let it dry out.
Rinse.

NEVER USE HEAT, NEVER USE ACIDS!

STAIN

BUGS

TYPE

protein

FORMULA

white vinegar or lemon juice
digestant

METHOD

Remove as much of the dead bug as possible. Rinse stain with a vinegar or lemon juice solution (half water). If necessary, moisten the stain and apply digestant paste; don't let it dry out. Remove the paste and wash garment, or in the case of nonwashables, rinse or sponge off stained area thoroughly.

STAIN

BUTTER

TYPE

grease

FORMULA

combination solvent
oil solvent
absorbent

METHOD

For washable fabrics, pretreat the stain with a combination solvent, then wash. If any stain remains after washing, let fabric dry and use an oil solvent to remove the remainder. For nonwashables, keep the fabric warm so the butter doesn't harden. Apply an absorbent and let it work for several hours, following with fresh absorbent if necessary. If any stain remains, spray with an oil solvent, let dry and brush off.

STAIN

CANDLE WAX

TYPE

dye, wax

FORMULA

boiling water or warm iron
white vinegar or lemon juice
bleach

METHOD

Remove as much of the wax as you can with a dull knife. Spread the stained area over a bowl, and pour boiling water through the fabric from a height of 12 inches. The hot water will melt the wax, and the force of the water will wash the stain into the bowl. If the fabric is non-washable or can't stand boiling water, sandwich the stain between two clean cloths or paper towels and press with a warm iron. If a colored stain remains, apply some vinegar or lemon juice, and wash garment. Bleach if necessary and possible.

STAIN

CARAMEL

TYPE

burnt sugar

FORMULA

combination solvent

METHOD

If fabric is washable, soak the garment in *warm* water to loosen the caramel. Apply a combination solvent to the stain and wash garment. For nonwashable fabrics, use *warm* water to loosen the caramel. If this is impossible, send garment to a dry cleaner.

NEVER USE HEAT ON A SUGAR STAIN!

STAIN

CARBON PAPER

TYPE

ink

FORMULA

ammonia
liquid soap
oil solvent

METHOD

Apply a few drops of ammonia to the stain, then apply liquid soap. Rinse thoroughly, then wash garment. For nonwashable fabrics, use an oil solvent. Spray the solvent on the stain, let dry and brush off.

STAIN

CAVIAR

TYPE

protein, dye

FORMULA

cool water
digestant

METHOD

There are two problems with caviar stains: wasting the caviar and removing the stains. Rinse with *cool* water to remove most of the stain. Apply digestant paste to stain—don't let it dry out. Rinse with *cool* water.

HOT WATER WILL SET A CAVIAR STAIN!

STAIN

CHARCOAL

TYPE

carbon, organic materials

FORMULA

liquid soap
ammonia

METHOD

To remove charcoal from clothes, moisten the stain with some water. Rub in some liquid soap and then add a few drops of ammonia. Rinse the stained area, then if fabric is washable, machine wash the entire garment in warm soapy water. If the fabric is nonwashable, sponge the stained area with plain water to remove liquid soap and ammonia.

STAIN

CHEESE SAUCE

TYPE

grease, coloring

FORMULA

combination solvent
digestant
oil solvent

METHOD

For washable fabrics, a simple method is to apply a combination solvent and wash garment in *cool* water. If any stain remains, moisten and apply digestant paste— don't let it dry out. Rinse. For nonwashable fabrics, remove as much residue as possible, sponge stain with warm water, let dry, then use an oil solvent. Spray the solvent on the stain, let dry and brush off.

STAIN

CHERRIES

TYPE

fruit

FORMULA

water
glycerin
combination solvent

METHOD

Immediately sponge off the stain with *cool* water. If the fabric is not fragile, use the boiling water method: Spread the stained area over a bowl, and pour boiling water through the fabric from a height of 12 inches. The hot water will set the stain, but not before the force of the water washes the stain into the bowl. If the fabric is nonwashable or can't stand boiling water, apply glycerin to stain, rinse, then treat with a combination solvent and rinse again.

NEVER USE SOAP AND NEVER IRON A FRUIT STAIN!

STAIN

TYPE

protein, grease

FORMULA

cool water
combination solvent
soapy water
oil solvent
digestant

METHOD

This is a combination stain: the fat from the chicken causes a greasy stain, and the meat causes a protein stain. Remove the nongreasy portion first by soaking the stain in *cool* water for up to 30 minutes. Spray with a combination solvent and rinse with soapy water. Rinse with plain water and let dry. If any stain remains, use an oil solvent. If this is not totally successful, apply digestant paste to the stain—don't let it dry out. Rinse. This will remove any residual protein stain.

STAIN

CHILI

TYPE

protein, grease, tomato

FORMULA

cool water
combination solvent
white vinegar
oil solvent

METHOD

There are dozens of varieties of chili. The stain will be different depending on whether you're eating chili con carne, Texas chili or vegetarian chili. The spiciness of the chili doesn't have much effect on the severity of the stain, however.

Rinse the stain with *cool* water. To remove the tomato portion of the stain, spray with a combination solvent, and rinse. If any tomato color remains, rinse stain with a vinegar solution (half water), and rinse again with cool water. Any remaining stain is from the grease in the meat. Let fabric dry and apply an oil solvent.

STAIN

TYPE

protein, grease, sugar

FORMULA

absorbent
oil solvent
digestant

METHOD

Next time, maybe you should try M&M's, which melt in your mouth.

Remove as much of the chocolate as you can, then apply an absorbent to soak up as much of the stain as possible. Apply an oil solvent. Any stain that remains after this is due to the protein. To remove, moisten stain and apply digestant paste—don't let it dry out. Rinse.

NEVER USE HEAT ON A SUGAR STAIN!

STAIN

TYPE

tannic acid, protein (sugar, fat)

FORMULA

combination solvent
glycerin
water
oil solvent
white vinegar

METHOD

An all too common stain, with many permutations in its removal: If there was sugar in the coffee, first apply a combination solvent to stain and rinse with *cool* water. For wool, silk and nonwashables, apply glycerin to stain and let stand for 30 minutes. Rinse out with *cool* water. For washable fabrics, sponge off with *cool* water, stretch the stained area over a bowl and pour boiling water through the fabric from a height of 12 inches. If there was cream or milk in the coffee, you will have to follow up either procedure with an oil solvent. Let fabric dry first. If any stain remains, try rinsing with a vinegar solution (half water), and rinse again with plain water.

NEVER USE HEAT ON A SUGAR STAIN!

47

STAIN

TYPE

alcohol, fruit

FORMULA

salt
boiling water
oil solvent
white vinegar

METHOD

For washable fabrics, stretch the stained area over a bowl, pour salt over the stain and pour boiling water through the fabric from a height of 12 inches. If the fabric can't take boiling water, pour salt on the stain, and moisten. Let stand for 20 minutes and scrape the salt off. Rinse. If these methods are too harsh for the fabric, use an oil solvent. If any stain remains, follow with a rinse of a vinegar solution (half water), and rinse again with plain water.

NEVER USE SOAP AND NEVER IRON A FRUIT STAIN!

STAIN

COLA

TYPE

sugar (12 tablespoons per can!), coloring, tannin

FORMULA

warm water
combination solvent
glycerin

METHOD

The "Real Thing" can really soil your clothes. Move very quickly to remove as much of the stain as possible. Immediately rinse with *warm* water. Apply a combination solvent, and wash. If the fabric can't be washed, apply glycerin and let stand for 30 minutes. Rinse.

NEVER USE HEAT ON A SUGAR STAIN!

STAIN

TYPE

oil, egg, vegetable, sour cream, sugar

FORMULA

absorbent
combination solvent
liquid soap
ammonia
oil solvent

METHOD

First, using an absorbent, remove as much of the stain as you can. If fabric is washable, and the stain is still visible, apply a combination solvent, then rinse. Apply some liquid soap, and rinse again. Finally, wash the garment.

If the stain is not visible, apply liquid soap and then wash. If the colors of the garment are affected, rinse with a mixture of ammonia and water, and rinse again with plain water. If the garment is not washable, use an oil solvent.

HEAT SETS EGG AND SUGAR STAINS!

STAIN

COLORED CHALK

TYPE

chalk, coloring, wax

FORMULA

oil solvent

METHOD

Brush off loose chalk. Use a damp cloth to remove as much of stain as possible. Let fabric dry. Follow with an oil solvent.

STAIN

CORN CHIPS (DORITOS, ETC.)

TYPE

vegetable oil, starch, coloring, salt

FORMULA

absorbent
combination solvent
petroleum jelly
oil solvent

METHOD

Brush off crumbs. Use an absorbent to remove as much of the grease as possible. (This works on carpets as well.) If the fabric is washable, apply a combination solvent and some petroleum jelly, and wash. Nonwashable fabrics should be treated with an oil solvent.

STAIN

CORRECTION FLUID (LIQUID PAPER, ETC.)

TYPE

synthetic solvent-based coating

FORMULA

acetone
oil solvent

METHOD

Scrape off as much of correction fluid as possible. If the fabric can take it, apply acetone, and rinse. Otherwise, try an oil solvent. Spray the solvent on the stain, let dry and brush off.

CAUTION: ACETONE IS EXTREMELY FLAMMABLE. DO NOT USE ACETONE ON FABRICS CONTAINING ACETATE OR TRIACETATE!

STAIN

COUGH MEDICINE

TYPE

sugar, dye, alcohol

FORMULA

absorbent
combination solvent
glycerin
digestant

METHOD

Using an absorbent, remove as much of the medicine as you can. Apply a combination solvent to stain and rinse with *cool* water. If fabric is washable, wash garment in *cool* water. If any stain remains, rinse with a glycerin solution (half water), then rinse again with plain water. If there is still residue, apply digestant paste while keeping the spot moist. Rinse.

NEVER USE HEAT ON A SUGAR STAIN!

STAIN

CRANBERRY JUICE

TYPE

fruit

FORMULA

water
glycerin
combination solvent

METHOD

Immediately sponge off the stain with *cool* water. If the fabric is not fragile, use the boiling water method: Spread the stained area over a bowl, and pour boiling water through the fabric from a height of 12 inches. The hot water will set the stain, but not before the force of the water washes the stain into the bowl. If the fabric can't stand boiling water, apply glycerin to stain, rinse, then apply a combination solvent, and wash garment. If the fabric is nonwashable, sponge the stained area with plain water to rinse.

NEVER USE SOAP AND NEVER IRON A FRUIT STAIN!

STAIN

CRAYON

TYPE

dye, wax

FORMULA

boiling water or warm iron
white vinegar or lemon juice
bleach

METHOD

Remove as much of crayon as you can with a dull knife. Spread the stained area over a bowl, and pour boiling water through the fabric from a height of 12 inches. The hot water will melt the wax, and the force of the water will wash the stain into the bowl. If the fabric is non-washable or can't stand boiling water, sandwich the stain between two clean cloths or paper towels, and press with a warm iron. If a colored stain remains, apply some vinegar or lemon juice, and rinse. Use bleach if necessary and fabric can stand it. Wash washables.

STAIN

DOG STAINS/PET EXCREMENT

TYPE

animal waste

FORMULA

combination solvent
detergent
white vinegar

METHOD

First, shoot the dog.

Remove as much of the evidence as possible with a dull blade. If fabric is washable, pretreat stain with a combination solvent and wash garment with detergent and water. Rinse well. If any stain remains, sponge with a water and vinegar solution. Rinse. If fabric is nonwashable, take to the dry cleaner!

STAIN

TYPE

grease

FORMULA

combination solvent
oil solvent
absorbent

METHOD

For washable fabrics, treat stain with a combination solvent, then wash garment. If any stain remains after washing, treat with an oil solvent when fabric is dry. For nonwashables, keep the fabric warm so the butter doesn't harden. Apply an absorbent and let it work for several hours, following with fresh absorbent if necessary. If any stain remains, use an oil solvent to remove it. Spray the solvent on the stain, let dry and brush off.

STAIN

EGG

TYPE

protein, grease

FORMULA

digestant

METHOD

Moisten the stain and apply digestant paste. Don't let the paste dry out. Rinse.

HEAT SETS EGG STAINS!

STAIN

EYESHADOW

TYPE

grease, wax, dye, coloring

FORMULA

combination solvent
bleach
oil solvent

METHOD

For washable fabrics, apply a combination solvent to stain and wash garment. If a stain remains, you may need to use some bleach. For nonwashable fabrics, spray an oil solvent on the stain, let dry and brush off.

STAIN

FISH

TYPE

protein

FORMULA

cool water
digestant
salt

METHOD

Sponge or rinse with *cool* water to remove most of the stain. Apply digestant paste to stain, keeping the paste moist with *cool* water. Sponge off or rinse with *cool* water. Remove the odor by rinsing with a saltwater solution (1/4 cup salt to 1 quart water), then with plain water. If fabric is nonwashable, sponge the stained area, first with saltwater solution, then plain water.

STAIN

FOOD COLORING

TYPE

vegetable dyes

FORMULA

glycerin
combination solvent
alcohol
white vinegar
digestant

METHOD

First, apply glycerin or combination solvent to stain. Let stand for 20 minutes, then rinse. If any stain remains, rinse with a mixture of half water, half alcohol and a few drops of vinegar. If the stain withstands all of this punishment, finish it off with an application of digestant paste (keep the paste moist). Rinse. If the fabric is non-washable, sponge the stained area instead of rinsing.

===

STAIN

FRENCH DRESSING

TYPE

oil, egg, sugar, tomato

FORMULA

absorbent
combination solvent
liquid detergent
ammonia
oil solvent

METHOD

Salad dressings cause a difficult combination of greasy and nongreasy stains. First, using an absorbent, remove as much of the stain as you can. If the fabric is washable, and the stain is visible, treat with a combination solvent, then rinse with *cool* water. Apply some liquid detergent, and rinse again. Finally, wash the garment.

If the stain is not visible, apply liquid detergent and then wash. If the colors of the garment are affected, wash with a mixture of ammonia and water. Rinse. If the garment is not washable, use an oil solvent.

NEVER USE HEAT ON A SUGAR STAIN!

STAIN

FURNITURE POLISH

TYPE

coloring, oil, wax

FORMULA

absorbent
oil solvent

METHOD

Use an absorbent to remove as much of the stain as possible. Follow this with an oil solvent.

STAIN

GASOLINE

TYPE

petroleum distillates and additives

FORMULA

combination solvent
oil solvent

METHOD

Self-service gas isn't always a bargain! If fabric is washable, treat stain with a combination solvent, and wash garment. For nonwashable fabrics, try an oil solvent. Spray the solvent on the stain, let dry and brush off.

STAIN

GLUE, ANIMAL

TYPE

protein, gelatin

FORMULA

digestant
ammonia

METHOD

Soak the stain in water to soften the glue. Remove as much as you can by rinsing, then apply digestant paste. Don't let it dry out. Rinse. If any stain remains, rinse with an ammonia solution (half water) and rinse again with plain water. If the garment is not washable, dry cleaning is your best alternative.

STAIN

GLUE, MUCILAGE (PASTE)

TYPE

vegetable, starch

FORMULA

water

METHOD

If garment is washable, soak the stained area in water to loosen the glue, then wash garment. If garment is nonwashable, take to a dry cleaner.

STAIN

GLUE, SYNTHETIC

TYPE

plastics

FORMULA

soap and water
white vinegar

METHOD

If the glue hasn't hardened, wash out with soap and water. Rinse. If fabric is nonwashable, sponge stained area with soapy water, then plain water to rinse.

If the glue has hardened, you can try this method: Make a solution of vinegar and water. Heat until near boiling. Immerse the affected area and let soak until the glue is loosened. (This may take up to 20 minutes.) Rinse. Wash garment. If the fabric is nonwashable, take garment to dry cleaner.

STAIN

GLUE, WHITE (ELMER'S)

TYPE

milk

FORMULA

water

METHOD

Soak stained area in the hottest water the fabric can stand. After a while the glue will soften and then it can be rinsed out. Machine wash washables.

STAIN

GRAPE JUICE

TYPE

fruit

FORMULA

water
glycerin
combination solvent

METHOD

Kids love grape juice. When they pour it all over your tablecloth, it looks like the stain will never come out. Don't panic, but work fast.

Immediately sponge off the stain with *cool* water. If the fabric is not fragile, use the boiling water method: Spread the stained area over a bowl, and pour boiling water through the fabric from a height of 12 inches. The hot water will set the stain, but not before the force of the water washes the stain into the bowl. If the fabric can't stand boiling water, apply glycerin to stain, rinse, then treat with a combination solvent, and wash garment, if washable.

If the fabric is nonwashable, sponge the stained area with *cool* water. Apply glycerin, then sponge off with *cool* water. Apply a combination solvent, and again sponge off with plain water to rinse.

NEVER USE SOAP AND NEVER IRON A FRUIT STAIN!

STAIN

TYPE

fruit

FORMULA

water
glycerin
combination solvent

METHOD

Immediately sponge off the stain with *cool* water. If the fabric is not fragile, use the boiling water method: Spread the stained area over a bowl, and pour boiling water through the fabric from a height of 12 inches. The hot water will set the stain, but not before the force of the water washes the stain into the bowl. If the fabric can't stand boiling water, apply glycerin to stain, rinse, then treat with a combination solvent, and wash garment.

If the fabric is nonwashable, sponge the stained area with *cool* water. Apply glycerin, then sponge off with *cool* water. Apply a combination solvent, and again sponge off with plain water to rinse.

NEVER USE SOAP AND NEVER IRON A FRUIT STAIN!

STAIN

GRASS

TYPE

vegetable dye

FORMULA

alcohol
white vinegar
bleach

METHOD

Sponge stain with alcohol. (Always test to make sure the alcohol won't hurt the fabric.) If this doesn't work, rinse with vinegar. If this very mild bleaching agent doesn't work, try using bleach, if fabric will stand it. Then wash garment. If the fabric is nonwashable, sponge the stained area with vinegar, then with plain water to rinse.

CAUTION: ALCOHOL IS EXTREMELY FLAMMABLE AND CAN MAKE COLORS RUN!

STAIN

GRAVY

TYPE

protein, animal fat, starch

FORMULA

absorbent
cool water
digestant
oil solvent

METHOD

Using an absorbent, remove as much of the stain as possible. If the fabric is washable, soak in *cool* water to loosen the starch stain. If any stain remains, moisten the fabric and apply digestant paste—don't let it dry out. Rinse. If the fabric is not washable, use an oil solvent. Spray the solvent on the stain, let dry and brush off.

STAIN

TYPE

grease, dirt

FORMULA

absorbent
combination solvent
petroleum jelly
oil solvent

METHOD

When you get lubricating grease on your clothes, the dirt and impurities it has picked up can make a real mess. First, use an absorbent to remove as much of the gunk as possible. (This works on carpets as well.) If the fabric is washable, apply a combination solvent and some petroleum jelly, and wash garment. Nonwashable fabrics should be treated with an oil solvent. Spray the solvent on the stain, let dry and brush off.

STAIN

GROUND-IN DIRT

TYPE

earth, mud

FORMULA

combination solvent
bleach
detergent
oil solvent

METHOD

For washable fabrics, pretreat the stain with a combination solvent. Wash—with bleach if possible. The combination solvent will loosen much of the dirt, and the bleach will remove the color of what remains. If fabric is nonwashable, spot clean with detergent in water and, when dry, with an oil solvent. Spray the solvent on the stain, let dry and brush off.

STAIN

TYPE

animal waste

FORMULA

combination solvent
detergent
white vinegar

METHOD

They say that it is good luck to get hit with bird drop-
pings. This isn't true, it was just made up to make you
feel better.

Remove as much of the guano as possible with a dull
blade. Treat stain with a combination solvent and wash
garment with detergent and water. If any stain remains,
apply a mixture of 50 percent water and 50 percent
vinegar solution, and rinse. If the garment is nonwashable, take to the dry cleaner!

STAIN

TYPE

tree rubber, sugar, coloring

FORMULA

peanut butter
oil solvent
combination solvent
hammer

METHOD

If the gum is in your hair or carpeting, soften with peanut butter and remove. You can remove any peanut butter stain with an oil solvent or a combination solvent, depending on the fabric.

If the gum is on a piece of clothing, you might try freezing it and shattering the frozen gum with a hammer. If this doesn't work, soften the gum with an oil solvent, remove as much as you can and repeat the process.

After the gum itself is removed, some sugar and coloring may remain. Rinse stained area well with *cool* water, treat with a combination solvent and machine wash garment. If the fabric is nonwashable, sponge the stained area with a mixture of combination solvent and *cool* water, then with plain water to rinse, or try an oil solvent.

DO NOT USE HEAT! DO NOT IRON A GUM STAIN!

STAIN

HAIR COLORING

TYPE

dye, iron, tannin, acid

FORMULA

glycerin
white vinegar
ammonia

METHOD

Soften the stain with glycerin. Apply some vinegar and rinse well. If any stain remains, apply some ammonia, rinse thoroughly and wash garment. If the fabric is nonwashable, after softening stain with glycerin, sponge the stained area with vinegar, then plain water to rinse.

Sponge with ammonia and again with water to remove any remaining stain.

STAIN

HAIR MOUSSE

TYPE

oil, alcohol, thickeners

FORMULA

combination solvent
white vinegar

METHOD

Sponge some water on stain. Apply combination solvent and a spoonful of vinegar. Rinse. Machine wash garment. If the fabric is nonwashable, sponge the stained area with a mixture of combination solvent and water and vinegar, then with plain water to rinse.

STAIN

HAIR SPRAY

TYPE

lacquer

FORMULA

alcohol
detergent

METHOD

Apply some alcohol. (Test on fabric first to be sure alcohol doesn't pull the dye.) Follow with a washing in detergent and water. If the fabric is nonwashable, sponge the stained area with a mixture of detergent and water, then with plain water to rinse.

CAUTION: ALCOHOL IS EXTREMELY FLAMMABLE AND CAN MAKE COLORS RUN!

STAIN

TYPE

vegetable dye

FORMULA

glycerin
combination solvent
alcohol
white vinegar
digestant

METHOD

First, apply glycerin or combination solvent to stain and let stand. Rinse. If any stain remains, rinse with a mixture of 50 percent water, 50 percent alcohol plus a few drops of vinegar. If the stain withstands all of this punishment, finish it off with an application of digestant paste. Don't let paste dry out. Rinse. If the fabric is nonwashable, sponge off the stained area instead of rinsing.

CAUTION: ALCOHOL IS EXTREMELY FLAMMABLE AND CAN MAKE COLORS RUN!

STAIN

HOISIN SAUCE

TYPE

fruit (plums), sugar, salt

FORMULA

water
glycerin
combination solvent

METHOD

Immediately sponge off the stain with *cool* water. If the fabric is not fragile, use the boiling water method: Spread the stained area over a bowl, and pour boiling water through the fabric from a height of 12 inches. The hot water will set the stain, but not before the force of the water washes the stain into the bowl. If the fabric is nonwashable or can't stand boiling water, apply glycerin to stain, sponge or rinse off, then treat with a combination solvent and again sponge off or rinse with plain water. Machine wash washables.

NEVER USE SOAP AND NEVER IRON A FRUIT STAIN!

NEVER USE HEAT ON A SUGAR STAIN!

STAIN

HOT FUDGE

TYPE

protein, grease, sugar

FORMULA

absorbent
oil solvent
digestant

METHOD

Remove as much of the fudge as you can, then apply
an absorbent to soak up as much of the stain as possible.
Brush off absorbent and apply an oil solvent. Any stain
that remains is due to the protein in the chocolate. Moist-
en stain and apply digestant paste—don't let it dry out.
Rinse.

NEVER USE HEAT ON A SUGAR STAIN!

STAIN

ICE CREAM

TYPE

fat, sugar, coloring, milk (possibly fruit, chocolate, etc.)

FORMULA

combination solvent
liquid soap
oil solvent

METHOD

The treatment you use depends on the flavor of the ice cream and the type of fabric stained. After you've removed the milk portion of the stain, you'll have to treat the stain left by the flavor—fruit or chocolate for example.

For washable fabrics, a simple method is to apply a combination solvent to stain and wash garment in *cool* water. For nonwashable fabrics, sponge stain with liquid soap in *cool* water, then with plain water to rinse. When fabric is dry, apply oil solvent to remove the grease stain.

Follow appropriate method (for chocolate, fruit, etc.) to remove any remaining stain.

NEVER USE HEAT ON A SUGAR STAIN!

81

STAIN

IRON SCORCH

TYPE

burn

FORMULA

brush or sandpaper
bleach

METHOD

If the scorch is severe, the fibers are ruined and the stain can't be removed. Synthetics are especially hard to repair.

Remove as many of the damaged fibers as you can with a brush or with fine sandpaper. Machine wash garment. After washing, carefully bleach any remaining scorch-marks and rinse thoroughly. If the fabric is nonwashable, sponge the stained area instead of washing.

STAIN

TYPE

oil, vegetable dyes

FORMULA

absorbent
combination solvent
liquid soap
ammonia
oil solvent

METHOD

Salad dressings cause a difficult combination of greasy and nongreasy stains. First, using an absorbent, remove as much of the stain as you can. If fabric is washable, and the stain is visible, apply a combination solvent to stain, then rinse. Apply some liquid soap and rinse again. Finally, wash the garment.

If the stain is not visible, apply liquid soap to stain and then wash. If the colors of the garment are affected, rinse with a mixture of ammonia and water. Rinse thoroughly with plain water.

83

If the garment is not washable, use an oil solvent. Spray the solvent on the stain, let dry and brush off.

STAIN

JELLY

TYPE

sugar, fruit

FORMULA

combination solvent
water
glycerin
white vinegar

METHOD

Remove as much of the jelly as you can with a dull blade. Rinse stained area with *cool* water. Apply a combination solvent and rinse again to remove the sugar stain. If any stain remains, it is caused by the fruit. If the fabric is not fragile, use the boiling water method: Spread the stained area over a bowl, and pour boiling water through the fabric from a height of 12 inches. The hot water will set the stain, but not before the force of the water washes the stain into the bowl. If the fabric can't stand boiling water, apply glycerin to stain, rinse, then treat with a combination solvent, and machine wash garment.

If fabric is nonwashable, sponge stained area with *cool* water, then with white vinegar, then sponge thoroughly with water to rinse.

NEVER USE HEAT ON A SUGAR STAIN!

NEVER USE SOAP AND NEVER IRON A FRUIT STAIN!

STAIN

KETCHUP

TYPE

tomato, sugar

FORMULA

cool water
combination solvent
white vinegar
digestant

METHOD

Rinse the stain with *cool* water. Spray with a combination solvent and rinse. If any tomato color remains,
rinse with a vinegar solution (half water) and rinse again
with plain water. If any stain is still visible, moisten and
apply a digestant paste—don't let it dry out. Rinse.

NEVER USE HEAT ON A SUGAR STAIN!

STAIN

LEMON JUICE

TYPE

bleach

FORMULA

water
glycerin
combination solvent

METHOD

Immediately sponge off the lemon juice with *cool* water.
If the fabric is not fragile, use the boiling water method:
Spread the stained area over a bowl, and pour boiling
water through the fabric from a height of 12 inches. The

hot water will set the stain, but not before the force of the water washes the stain into the bowl. If the fabric can't stand boiling water, apply glycerin to stain, rinse, then treat with a combination solvent, and wash garment. If the fabric is nonwashable, keep treated area damp for 10 minutes and then rinse.

NEVER USE SOAP AND NEVER IRON A FRUIT STAIN!

STAIN

LIPSTICK

TYPE

dye, grease, wax

FORMULA

oil solvent
liquid soap
ammonia

METHOD

Apply an oil solvent to stain. Rinse. Repeat the process on any remaining stain. If the stain persists, treat with a few drops of liquid soap mixed with ammonia, and rinse.

STAIN

MARGARINE

TYPE

grease, coloring

FORMULA

absorbent
combination solvent
petroleum jelly
oil solvent

METHOD

First, use an absorbent to remove as much of the grease
as possible. (This works on carpets as well.) If the fabric
is washable, apply a combination solvent and some petroleum jelly, and wash. Nonwashable fabrics should be
treated with an oil solvent. Spray the solvent on the stain,
let dry and brush off.

STAIN

MARKER INK (MAGIC MARKER, ETC.)

TYPE

dye

FORMULA

glycerin
combination solvent
ammonia
bleach
alcohol
hydrogen peroxide

METHOD

Each ink formulation is different. It is possible that your stain is permanent. However, try this method before panicking: Apply glycerin to stain and let stand for 30 minutes. Mix combination solvent with a few drops of ammonia and apply to the stain. Machine wash garment. If any stain remains, try bleach.

If the fabric is nonwashable, sponge the stained area with alcohol followed by hydrogen peroxide. Rinse or sponge off with plain water.

STAIN

MASCARA

TYPE

grease, wax

FORMULA

combination solvent
bleach
oil solvent

METHOD

If fabric is washable, apply a combination solvent to stain, and wash garment. If any stain remains, you may need to use some bleach. For nonwashable fabrics, apply an oil solvent. Spray the solvent on the stain, let dry and brush off.

STAIN

MASHED POTATOES

TYPE

starch, fat

FORMULA

cool water
absorbent
combination solvent
oil solvent
digestant

METHOD

Plain potato is easy to get out—rinse fabric with *cool* water to remove the starch stain. Once you add butter or sour cream, the stain problem gets worse.

Scrape off as much of the potato as possible. For washable fabrics, apply an absorbent to the stain and let it work. Soak garment in *cool* water to loosen the starch stain. Then apply a combination solvent to stain and wash the garment. If any stain remains, when fabric is dry use an oil solvent to remove the remainder of the stain. Spray solvent on the stain, let dry and brush off. For nonwashables, apply an absorbent, and let it work for several hours. Follow with fresh absorbent. If any stain remains, treat with an oil solvent.

To remove any remaining stain, moisten the fabric and apply digestant paste. Don't let paste dry out. Rinse.

STAIN

TYPE

oil, egg

FORMULA

absorbent
combination solvent
liquid soap
ammonia
oil solvent

METHOD

First, using an absorbent, remove as much of the stain
as you can. If fabric is washable, and the stain is visible,
apply a combination solvent, then rinse. Apply some
liquid soap and rinse again. Finally, wash the garment.

If the stain is not visible, use liquid soap and then wash.
If the colors of the garment are affected, rinse with a
mixture of ammonia and water. Rinse again with plain
water.

If the garment is not washable, use an oil solvent. Spray
the solvent on the stain, let dry and brush off.

STAIN

MELON

TYPE

fruit

FORMULA

water
glycerin
combination solvent
white vinegar

METHOD

Immediately sponge off the stain with *cool* water. If the fabric is not fragile, use the boiling water method: Spread the stained area over a bowl, and pour boiling water through the fabric from a height of 12 inches. The hot water will set the stain, but not before the force of the water washes the stain into the bowl. If the fabric can't stand boiling water, apply glycerin to stain, rinse, then treat with a combination solvent and wash garment.

If fabric is nonwashable, sponge stain off with *cool* water. Apply vinegar solution, then rinse.

NEVER USE SOAP AND NEVER IRON A FRUIT STAIN!

STAIN

TYPE

poisonous fungus

FORMULA

chlorine bleach
liquid soap

METHOD

Chlorine bleach kills mildew on contact—use it full strength on nonfabric surfaces. (Be sure to wear gloves.)

If the garment is washable, add a little chlorine bleach to some soapy water and wash thoroughly. If you use a small amount of bleach, it shouldn't affect the color of the garment, but test first to be sure. If the mildew is severe, it may have damaged the fabric. Brush off as much mildew as you can (outdoors) and then wash garment with bleach and water as above. Nonwashable fabrics should be dry-cleaned.

STAIN

MILK

TYPE

butterfat, water

FORMULA

digestant
detergent
oil solvent

METHOD

For washable fabrics, moisten the spot and apply digestant paste. Don't let it dry out. Rinse. For nonwashable fabrics, sponge stain with detergent and *cool* water, then plain water to rinse. Let dry and treat with an oil solvent.

STAIN

MOISTURIZER

TYPE

grease, mineral oil, coloring, perfume

FORMULA

absorbent
combination solvent
petroleum jelly
white vinegar
oil solvent

METHOD

First, use an absorbent to remove as much of the grease as possible. (This works on carpets as well.) If the fabric is washable, apply a combination solvent and some petroleum jelly, and wash garment. If any stain remains, apply some vinegar. Rinse.

Nonwashable fabrics should be treated with an oil solvent. Spray the solvent on the stain, let dry and brush off.

STAIN

MR. CLEAN

TYPE

ammonia, cleaning agents

FORMULA

cool water

METHOD

Rinse with lots of *cool* water.

STAIN

MUCUS

TYPE

protein

FORMULA

liquid soap
ammonia
digestant
detergent

METHOD

If fabric is washable, try to remove the stain by sponging
with a solution of 1 teaspoon liquid soap to 1 part water
to 2 tablespoons ammonia. Rinse. If this doesn't remove
the stain, moisten spot and apply digestant paste. Don't
let it dry out. Rinse. For nonwashable fabrics, sponge
with detergent and *cool* water, then plain water to rinse.

STAIN

MUSTARD

TYPE

mustard seed, vinegar, coloring, salt, sugar

FORMULA

liquid soap
absorbent
glycerin
alcohol

METHOD

For washable fabrics, apply liquid soap to stain, and machine wash garment in *cool* water. For nonwashable fabrics, use an absorbent to remove as much of stain as possible. Sponge on some glycerin and let stand for 30 minutes. Rinse, then apply a mixture of water and alcohol. Rinse again.

CAUTION: ALCOHOL IS EXTREMELY FLAMMABLE AND CAN MAKE COLORS RUN!

DO NOT USE ALKALI BLEACH ON A MUSTARD STAIN!

NEVER USE HEAT ON A SUGAR STAIN!

STAIN

NAIL POLISH

TYPE

cellulose acetate, dye

FORMULA

acetone

METHOD

Always test carefully to be sure the acetone won't damage the fabric. Rinse stain with acetone and wash garment. If the fabric is nonwashable or can't take acetone, consult a dry cleaner.

DO NOT USE NAIL POLISH REMOVER—IT STAINS!

CAUTION: ACETONE IS EXTREMELY FLAMMABLE. DO NOT USE ACETONE ON FABRICS CONTAINING ACETATE OR TRIACETATE!

STAIN

NAIL POLISH REMOVER

TYPE

acetone, perfume, stabilizer, oil

FORMULA

acetone

METHOD

Remember to test carefully to be sure the acetone won't damage the fabric. Rinse stain with acetone and wash garment. If the fabric is nonwashable or can't take acetone, take the garment to the dry cleaner.

CAUTION: ACETONE IS EXTREMELY FLAMMABLE. DO NOT USE ACETONE ON FABRICS CONTAINING ACETATE OR TRIACETATE!

STAIN

TYPE

pigment, oil

FORMULA

combination solvent
oil solvent

METHOD

If fabric is washable, apply combination solvent to stain
and wash garment. If fabric is nonwashable, try an oil
solvent. Spray the solvent on the stain, let dry and brush
off.

STAIN

NUTS

TYPE

vegetable oil, salt, coloring, sugar

FORMULA

absorbent
combination solvent
petroleum jelly
oil solvent

METHOD

First, use an absorbent to remove as much of the grease as possible. (This works on carpets as well.) If the fabric is washable, apply combination solvent and some petroleum jelly to stain and wash garment. Nonwashable fabrics should be treated with an oil solvent. Spray the solvent on the stain, let dry and brush off.

STAIN

OIL, MACHINE OR MOTOR

TYPE

oil, dirt

FORMULA

absorbent
combination solvent
petroleum jelly
oil solvent

METHOD

Motor oil runs through an engine to lubricate it and remove dirt and impurities. When you get the sludge on your clothes, the dirt and impurities can make a real mess. Machine oil is often dirty too. First, use an absorbent to remove as much of the oil as possible. (This works on carpets as well.) If the fabric is washable, apply a combination solvent and some petroleum jelly to the stain, and wash. Nonwashable fabrics should be treated with an oil solvent.

STAIN

ONION DIP

TYPE

oil, vegetable dye

FORMULA

absorbent
combination solvent
liquid soap
ammonia
oil solvent

METHOD

First, using an absorbent, remove as much of the stain as you can. If fabric is washable, and the stain is visible, apply a combination solvent, then rinse with *cool* water. Apply some liquid soap and rinse again. Finally, wash the garment.

If the stain is not visible, apply liquid soap and then wash garment. If the colors of the garment are affected, rinse with a mixture of 1 tablespoon ammonia to 1 cup water. Rinse with plain water. If the garment is not washable, try an oil solvent. Spray the solvent on the stain, let dry and brush off.

STAIN

ORANGE JUICE

TYPE

fruit

FORMULA

water
glycerin
combination solvent
white vinegar

METHOD

Immediately sponge off the stain with *cool* water. If the fabric is not fragile, use the boiling water method: Spread the stained area over a bowl, and pour boiling water through the fabric from a height of 12 inches. The hot water will set the stain, but not before the force of the water washes the stain into the bowl. If the fabric can't stand boiling water, apply glycerin to stain, rinse, then treat with a combination solvent and wash garment.

If fabric is nonwashable, sponge stain with vinegar solution, then with plain water to rinse.

NEVER USE SOAP AND NEVER IRON A FRUIT STAIN!

STAIN

ORANGE SODA

TYPE

coloring, sugar, flavoring

FORMULA

water
glycerin
combination solvent
white vinegar

METHOD

Immediately sponge off the stain with *cool* water. If the fabric is not fragile, use the boiling water method: Spread the stained area over a bowl, and pour boiling water through the fabric from a height of 12 inches. The hot water will set the stain, but not before the force of the water washes the stain into the bowl. If the fabric can't stand boiling water, apply glycerin to stain, rinse, then apply a combination solvent, and wash garment.

If fabric is nonwashable, sponge stain with vinegar solution, then with plain water to rinse.

NEVER USE SOAP AND NEVER IRON A FRUIT STAIN!

STAIN

PAINT, LATEX (WET)

TYPE

pigment, vehicle

FORMULA

water
oil solvent
combination solvent

METHOD

If you've spilled latex paint, you can minimize the damage by moving quickly. First, remove as much of the paint as possible by blotting it with a dry rag. Don't rub, as this will force the paint into the fabric. Next, use a damp sponge to soak up more of the paint. Once the sponge is wet with paint, wash it off, wring it out and start again. After you've removed as much paint as possible, rinse the fabric (if it is washable). Any paint that remains can be removed with an oil solvent. If the fabric isn't washable, apply a combination solvent, then follow with an oil solvent.

STAIN

PAINT, OIL OR LATEX (DRY)

TYPE

pigments, hardened polymer

FORMULA

paint remover
glycerin
combination solvent
oil solvent

METHOD

The hardest part is removing the chunks of dried-on paint. Apply paint remover and let the paint soften. Gently pry the surface paint off with a spatula. Repeat this process if necessary. If some paint still remains, apply glycerin and let stand for several hours. Then remove with a spatula. Treat any remaining stain with combination solvent, then oil solvent. Rinse. Machine wash garment. If the fabric is nonwashable, sponge or rinse the stained area instead of washing garment.

STAIN

PAINT, OIL (WET)

TYPE

pigments, dyes, oil

FORMULA

turpentine
oil solvent

METHOD

Using a dry rag, remove as much of the wet paint as possible. Don't rub or the paint will be forced into the fabric. Apply turpentine and rinse out as much paint as possible. Remove the rest of the stain with an oil solvent.

STAIN

PASTE, PAPER

TYPE

starch

FORMULA

water

METHOD

If garment is washable, soak in *cool* water to loosen the stain, then wash. If garment is nonwashable, it's best to take it to a dry cleaner.

STAIN

PEA SOUP

TYPE

fat, vegetable dye, protein

FORMULA

cool water
combination solvent
soapy water
oil solvent
digestant

METHOD

This is a combination stain, with the fat from the stock causing a greasy stain and the meat or vegetables causing a protein stain.

Remove the nongreasy portion first by soaking the stain in *cool* water for up to 30 minutes. Spray with a combination solvent and rinse with soapy water. Rinse with clear water and let dry.

If any stain remains, treat with an oil solvent. If this is not totally successful, moisten stain and apply digestant paste—don't let it dry out. Rinse. This will remove any remaining protein stain.

STAIN

PEANUT BUTTER

TYPE

grease, sugar, protein

FORMULA

combination solvent
digestant

METHOD

Apply a combination solvent to stain and rinse with *cool* water. If any stain remains, moisten and apply digestant paste. Don't let it dry out. Rinse. This should remove the remainder of the stain.

NEVER USE HEAT ON A SUGAR STAIN!

STAIN

PEN INK—BLUE OR BLACK

TYPE

pigment

FORMULA

hair spray
combination solvent

METHOD

Have patience. This is among the most difficult stains to remove. The secret here is to test the method first. If possible, put some of the same ink on a similar scrap of cloth and try any method of removal there first.

Method 1: Place a paper towel under the fabric and spray stain with ordinary hair spray. The hair spray will penetrate through the fabric and carry the ink with it. If the hair spray leaves a stain, remove according to instructions on page 77.

Method 2: Apply a combination solvent to stain and rinse with water.

STAIN

PENCIL

TYPE

graphite

FORMULA

eraser
liquid soap
ammonia
oil solvent

METHOD

Believe it or not, the best way to remove a pencil stain
is to erase it. Use a clean standard pencil eraser and rub
gently. (A kneaded rubber eraser, available from an art
supply store, works even better.) If the fabric can't take
this, or it doesn't work, for a washable fabric, apply a
few drops of liquid soap with some ammonia. Rinse
thoroughly and then wash garment. Use an oil solvent
on nonwashable fabrics.

STAIN

PERFUME

TYPE

oil, alcohol

FORMULA

glycerin
white vinegar

METHOD

Moisten the stain and apply some glycerin. Rinse with water. If any stain remains, apply a mild vinegar and water solution, and rinse with plain water.

STAIN

PINEAPPLE

TYPE

fruit

FORMULA

water
glycerin
combination solvent
white vinegar

METHOD

Immediately sponge off the stain with *cool* water. If the fabric is not fragile, use the boiling water method: Spread the stained area over a bowl, and pour boiling water through the fabric from a height of 12 inches. The hot water will set the stain, but not before the force of the water washes the stain into the bowl. If the fabric can't stand boiling water, apply glycerin to stain, rinse, then apply a combination solvent, and wash garment.

For nonwashables, sponge stained area with *cool* water, then with white vinegar. Rinse.

NEVER USE SOAP AND NEVER IRON A FRUIT STAIN!

STAIN

POLLEN

TYPE

vegetable dye

FORMULA

alcohol
white vinegar
bleach

METHOD

Sponge stain with alcohol. (Always test to make sure the alcohol won't hurt the fabric.) If this doesn't work, rinse with white vinegar. If this very mild bleaching agent doesn't work, and fabric is washable, try using a commercial bleach. Then wash garment.

CAUTION: ALCOHOL IS EXTREMELY FLAMMABLE AND CAN MAKE COLORS RUN!

STAIN

POTATO CHIPS

TYPE

starch, oil, salt

FORMULA

absorbent
combination solvent
petroleum jelly
oil solvent

METHOD

Brush off crumbs. Use an absorbent to remove as much of the grease as possible. (This works on carpets as well.)

If the fabric is washable, apply a combination solvent and some petroleum jelly to stain and wash garment. Nonwashable fabrics should be treated with an oil solvent. Spray the solvent on the stain, let dry and brush off.

STAIN

RELISH

TYPE

vegetable dye, oil, tomato, sugar

FORMULA

cool water
combination solvent
white vinegar
digestant

METHOD

Rinse the stain with *cool* water. Spray with a combination solvent, and rinse. If any tomato color remains, rinse with a vinegar solution (half water) and rinse again. If any stain is still visible, apply digestant paste. Don't let it dry out. Rinse.

NEVER USE HEAT ON A SUGAR STAIN!

STAIN

TYPE

enzymes, dirt, oils

FORMULA

combination solvent
bleach

METHOD

Believe it or not, Wisk is not the only answer to ring around the collar. The dirty halo on your collar is caused by sweat, dirt and oils mixing together. Treat the stain with a combination solvent, then wash garment, with bleach if colors will not be affected.

STAIN

ROOT BEER

TYPE

sugar, flavorings, tannin

118

FORMULA

combination solvent
glycerin

METHOD

Immediately remove as much of the stain as possible by rinsing with *warm* water. Apply a combination solvent, and wash garment. If the fabric can't be washed, apply glycerin to stain and let stand for 30 minutes. Rinse.

NEVER USE HEAT ON A SUGAR STAIN!

STAIN

ROSIN

TYPE

tree sap

FORMULA

oil solvent
detergent

METHOD

Use an oil solvent to loosen the rosin. Rinse. Wash garment with detergent and water, if washable.

STAIN

TYPE

oil, vegetable dyes, tomato, sugar, egg

FORMULA

absorbent
combination solvent
liquid detergent
ammonia
oil solvent

METHOD

Salad dressings cause a difficult combination of greasy
and nongreasy stains. First, using an absorbent, remove
as much of the stain as you can. If fabric is washable,
and the stain is visible, apply a combination solvent,
then rinse. Apply some liquid detergent, and rinse again.
Finally, wash the garment.

If the stain is not visible, apply liquid detergent and then
wash. If the colors of the garment are affected, wash
with a mixture of 1 tablespoon ammonia to 1 cup water.
If the garment is not washable, use an oil solvent. Spray
the solvent on the stain, let dry and brush off.

STAIN

TYPE

oxidized iron

FORMULA

salt
white vinegar
lemon juice
cream of tartar

METHOD

Washable fabrics:

Method 1: Make a paste of salt and vinegar. Rub the paste into the stain and let stand for 30 minutes. Wash garment.

Method 2: Apply a mixture of salt and lemon juice, and let dry in the sun. Rinse.

Method 3: Boil garment in a mixture of 1 quart water and 8 teaspoons of cream of tartar (more solution for larger garments). Rinse.

Method 4: Try washing garment with bleach.

Nonwashable fabrics: Take to the dry cleaner.

STAIN

TYPE

alcohol, coloring

FORMULA

cool water
liquid detergent
bleach

METHOD

Move quickly and sponge up as much of the stain as possible with *cool* water. If fabric is washable, soak in *cool* water for up to 12 hours to remove most of the stain. Rub liquid detergent into the stain, and wash garment. If fabric is nonwashable, rinse stain with *cool* water. If any stain remains, you'll have to use bleach or send garment out for professional cleaning.

STAIN

TYPE

protein

FORMULA

liquid soap
ammonia
digestant
liquid detergent

METHOD

If fabric is washable, try to remove the stain by sponging on a liquid soap-water-ammonia solution of 1 teaspoon soap to 1 part water to 2 tablespoons ammonia. Rinse. If this doesn't remove the stain, apply digestant paste. Don't let it dry out. Rinse. If fabric is nonwashable, sponge stain with detergent and *cool* water. Rinse.

STAIN

SHAVING CREAM

TYPE

fats, creams

FORMULA

detergent
oil solvent

METHOD

If the fabric is washable, moisten stain with a solution of detergent and water, then wash garment. For non-washable fabrics, try an oil solvent. Spray the solvent on the stain, let dry and brush off.

STAIN

SHERBET

TYPE

sugar, fat, fruit

FORMULA

combination solvent
glycerin
white vinegar

METHOD

With a dry cloth remove as much of the sherbet as possible. For washable fabrics, apply a combination solvent
and wash in *cool* water. If any stain remains, it is from
the fruit. If the fabric is not fragile, use the boiling water
method: Spread the stained area over a bowl, and pour
boiling water through the fabric from a height of 12
inches. The hot water will set the stain, but not before
the force of the water washes the stain into the bowl.
If the fabric can't stand boiling water, apply glycerin to
stain, rinse, then apply combination solvent, and wash
garment. If fabric is nonwashable, sponge stain with
vinegar solution, then with plain water to rinse.

NEVER USE HEAT ON A SUGAR STAIN!

*NEVER USE SOAP AND NEVER IRON A FRUIT
STAIN!*

STAIN

SHOE POLISH

TYPE

oil, wax, coloring

FORMULA

combination solvent
liquid soap
oil solvent

METHOD

For washable fabrics, apply a combination solvent to
stain. This will dissolve the shoe polish. Gently blot with
some clean paper towels, taking care not to rub the stain
into the fabric. Repeat the process until you've removed
as much stain as possible. Rub in some liquid soap, and
wash garment. For nonwashable fabrics, use an oil solvent. Spray the solvent on the stain, let dry and brush
off.

STAIN

SMOKE

TYPE

soot, resins

FORMULA

combination solvent
liquid soap
oil solvent

METHOD

If the fabric is washable, apply a combination solvent to stain. Rub in some liquid soap, and wash garment. For nonwashable fabrics, use an oil solvent.

STAIN

SOAP

TYPE

soap, perfume

FORMULA

warm water
white vinegar

METHOD

Rinse stain with *warm* water. It is unlikely that any soap you are using contains a harmful dye, but you may en-counter perfume. If the warm water doesn't remove the odor, apply a 50 percent vinegar and 50 percent water solution, and rinse.

STAIN

TYPE

butterfat

FORMULA

cool water
combination solvent
oil solvent
absorbent

METHOD

For washable fabrics, sponge off stain with *cool* water. Apply a combination solvent to stain, then wash garment. If any stain remains after washing, use an oil solvent to remove the remainder of the stain.

For nonwashables, apply an absorbent and let it work for several hours. Follow with fresh absorbent. If the stain remains, follow with an oil solvent. Spray the solvent on the stain, let dry and brush off.

STAIN

SOY SAUCE

TYPE

starch, salt, caramel coloring, sugar

FORMULA

cool water
combination solvent
white vinegar
oil solvent

METHOD

Confucius say: Next time, use a fork—chopsticks too messy.

Rinse stain with *cool* water. Apply a combination solvent, and wash garment. If any stain remains, apply vinegar, and rinse. For nonwashable fabrics, use an oil solvent. May require professional dry cleaning.

NEVER USE HEAT ON A SUGAR STAIN!

STAIN

TYPE

vegetable dye

FORMULA

water
glycerin
combination solvent
digestant

METHOD

Move quickly or the stain will set. Wash the stain in *cool* water, then apply glycerin and a combination solvent. Let sit for 5 minutes, then rinse. If any stain remains, apply digestant paste. Don't let it dry out. Rinse.

STAIN

TYPE

sugar, fruit

FORMULA

water
combination solvent
glycerin
white vinegar

METHOD

Scrape off as much of the jam as you can. Rinse and
then wash garment with *cool* water and a combination
solvent to remove the sugar stain. If any stain remains,
it is caused by the fruit.

If the fabric is not fragile, use the boiling water method:
Spread the stained area over a bowl, and pour boiling
water through the fabric from a height of 12 inches. The
hot water will set the stain, but not before the force of
the water washes the stain into the bowl. If the fabric
can't stand boiling water, apply glycerin to stain, rinse,
then treat with a combination solvent, and wash gar-

131

ment. For nonwashables, sponge stain with white vinegar, then rinse or sponge off with water.

NEVER USE HEAT ON A SUGAR STAIN!

NEVER USE SOAP AND NEVER IRON A FRUIT STAIN!

STAIN

STYLING GEL

TYPE

vegetable gums

FORMULA

detergent
lemon juice

METHOD

This product is water soluble, so a solution of detergent and water should remove the stain. If there is any discoloration remaining, treat with 1 teaspoon lemon juice to 1/4 cup water. Rinse with plain water.

STAIN

SUNTAN LOTION

TYPE

mineral oil, coloring, perfume, PABA

FORMULA

absorbent
combination solvent
petroleum jelly
white vinegar
oil solvent

METHOD

First, use an absorbent to remove as much of the grease as possible. (This works on carpets as well.) If the fabric is washable, apply a combination solvent and some petroleum jelly to stain and wash garment. If any color remains, apply some vinegar. Nonwashable fabrics should be treated with an oil solvent. Spray the solvent on the stain, let dry and brush off.

STAIN

SWEAT

TYPE

enzymes, salt, water

FORMULA

ammonia
white vinegar
oil solvent
chlorine bleach
salt

METHOD

Perspiration weakens a fabric and will eventually destroy it. Ironing a fabric discolored by perspiration stains will further aggravate the problem.

Sponge off fresh stains with a solution of 1 tablespoon ammonia to 1/2 cup water, then with vinegar, if necessary. Rinse. If an oily stain remains, use an oil solvent. Spray the solvent on the stain, let dry and brush off. If the area has yellowed, and the fabric will stand it, wash with bleach. This should remove the stain.

To remove odors that remain after washing, soak the garment in a gallon of *warm* water in which several spoonfuls of salt have been dissolved.

STAIN

SYRUP (PANCAKE)

TYPE

sugar, coloring, tree sap

FORMULA

warm water
liquid soap
combination solvent

METHOD

First, scrape off as much of the syrup as you can with a dull blade. Rinse or sponge stained area thoroughly with *warm* water until all of the sticky residue is gone. Wash washables. Send nonwashables to dry cleaner if necessary.

Once you have removed the sugar stain, treat any remaining stain with liquid soap or a combination solvent, and wash garment.

NEVER USE HEAT ON A SUGAR STAIN!

STAIN

TAR

TYPE

asphalt, dyes, many other components

FORMULA

glycerin
combination solvent
oil solvent

METHOD

Use a spatula to remove as much of the tar as possible.
Apply glycerin to soften the stain. For washable fabrics,
apply a combination solvent to the stain, and rinse. Repeat until the stain is gone. For nonwashable fabrics,
treat with an oil solvent until the stain is gone—you
may have to use several applications.

*DO NOT WASH THE FABRIC UNTIL THE STAIN
IS REMOVED!*

STAIN

TARTAR SAUCE

TYPE

oil, egg, relish

FORMULA

absorbent
combination solvent
liquid soap
ammonia
oil solvent

METHOD

First, using an absorbent, remove as much of the stain as you can. If fabric is washable, and the stain is visible, apply a combination solvent, then rinse. Apply some liquid soap and rinse again. Finally, wash the garment.

If the stain is not visible, apply liquid soap and then wash garment. If the colors of the garment are affected, rinse with a mixture of 2 tablespoons ammonia to 1 cup water. Rinse with plain water. If the garment is not washable, use an oil solvent. Spray the solvent on the stain, let dry and brush off.

STAIN

TEA

TYPE

tannic acid, protein (sugar, fat)

FORMULA

glycerin
water
combination solvent
oil solvent
white vinegar

METHOD

An all too common stain, with many permutations in its removal: for wool, silk and nonwashables, apply glycerin to stain and let stand for 30 minutes. Rinse out with *cool* water.

For washable fabrics that can stand hot water, stretch the stained area over a bowl and pour boiling water through the fabric from a height of 12 inches. If there was sugar in the tea, treat the stain with *cool* water and a combination solvent before exposure to boiling water. If there was milk in the tea, you will have to follow either procedure with an oil solvent. If any stain remains, try rinsing with a vinegar solution (half water), then with plain water.

NEVER USE HEAT ON A SUGAR STAIN!

STAIN

TOMATO

TYPE

fruit

FORMULA

cool water
combination solvent
white vinegar

METHOD

Rinse the stain with *cool* water. Spray with a combination solvent, and rinse. If any tomato color remains, apply a vinegar solution (half water), and rinse again.

NEVER USE SOAP AND NEVER IRON A FRUIT STAIN!

STAIN

TOOTHPASTE

TYPE

soap, flavoring, coloring

FORMULA

cool water
detergent
white vinegar
oil solvent

METHOD

For washable fabrics, rinse stain with *cool* water. Apply a mixture of detergent and water, and rinse. If any stain remains, apply vinegar and water, and wash garment. For nonwashable fabrics, try an oil solvent. Spray on stain, let dry and brush off.

STAIN

TREE SAP

TYPE

resins

FORMULA

oil solvent
detergent

METHOD

Use an oil solvent to remove the sap. Spray solvent on stain, let dry and brush off. If fabric is washable, launder with detergent.

STAIN

URINE

TYPE

acids, salts, pigments

FORMULA

cool water
ammonia
white vinegar or lemon juice
digestant

METHOD

Rinse the stain with *cool* water. Work in a few drops of ammonia, and rinse again. Work in some vinegar or lemon juice and let stand for 10 minutes, then rinse well. If this doesn't work, moisten the stain and apply digestant paste. Don't let it dry out. Rinse. Wash garment, if washable.

STAIN

VOMIT

TYPE

acids, enzymes

FORMULA

ammonia
liquid soap
water
digestant

METHOD

Vomit can permanently discolor fabrics, so it is important to remove it as soon as possible. The enzymes in
vomit are very powerful and will probably damage very
delicate fabrics. If this occurs, the fabric can't be saved.

Rinse the stained area thoroughly with *cool* water and
remove as much of the stain as possible. Rinse with a
solution of 2 tablespoons ammonia and 1 teaspoon liquid
soap to 1 pint water. Wash garment, if washable, or
rinse. If a stain remains, apply digestant paste to the
moistened stain. Don't let it dry out; rinse. Wash garment, if washable.

STAIN

WATER

TYPE

water

FORMULA

water

METHOD

Dampen the entire garment by holding it over a steaming kettle. (Don't burn fabric!) Place the fabric between two clean towels and iron while damp.

STAIN

WINDOW CLEANER (WINDEX, ETC.)

TYPE

detergent, alcohol, water, ammonia, coloring

FORMULA

cool water
white vinegar

METHOD

Rinse stain with *cool* water. If any stain remains, apply a vinegar and water mixture in equal proportions, and rinse. Wash garment, if washable.

STAIN

WINE

TYPE

alcohol, fruit, sugar

FORMULA

water
salt
oil solvent
white vinegar

METHOD

Sponge off stain with *cool* water. For washable fabrics, stretch the stained area over a bowl, pour salt over the stain and pour boiling water through the fabric from a height of 12 inches. If the fabric can't take boiling water, pour salt on the stain and moisten. Let stand, then scrape the salt off, and rinse. If these methods are too harsh for the fabric or it is nonwashable, use an oil solvent. If any stain remains, apply a vinegar solution (half water), and rinse.

NEVER USE HEAT ON A SUGAR STAIN!

NEVER USE SOAP AND NEVER IRON A FRUIT STAIN!

STAIN

TYPE

fat, enzymes, fruit

FORMULA

combination solvent
water
oil solvent
glycerin
absorbent

METHOD

For washable fabrics, apply a combination solvent to stain, then rinse with *cool* water. Let dry. If any stain remains, use an oil solvent to remove it.

If any fruit stain remains after removing the yogurt stain, you must treat that as well. If the fabric is not fragile, use the boiling water method: Spread the stained area over a bowl, and pour boiling water through the fabric from a height of 12 inches. The hot water will set the stain, but not before the force of the water washes the stain into the bowl. If the fabric can't stand boiling water, apply glycerin to stain, rinse, then apply a combination solvent, and wash garment.

For nonwashables, apply an absorbent and let it work for several hours. Follow with fresh absorbent if necessary. If any stain remains, treat with an oil solvent. Spray on, let dry and brush off.

NEVER USE SOAP AND NEVER IRON A FRUIT STAIN!

Appendix

COMMON STAIN REMOVERS

Absorbents
corn meal
cornstarch
talcum powder

Bleaches
ammonia
chlorine
hydrogen peroxide
lemon juice
synthetic bleaches
   Clorox II
   Snowy
white vinegar (acetic acid)

Combination Solvents
Magic
Shout
Spray 'n Wash

Digestants (enzyme paste)
amylase

Axion (laundry presoak)
Biz (laundry presoak)
papain
pepsin

Oil Solvents
Carbona Spot Remover
K2r

Pure Soaps
Ivory
Lux
Woolite

Index

151

About the Author

Herb Barndt, associate professor of textiles at the Philadelphia College of Textiles and Science (PCT&S), has created a number of courses in the curriculum at PCT&S for the more than 1,000 students trained there in textiles technology each year. Professor Barndt is director of the Grundy Center for Textile Product Evaluation, where he and his staff run the Stain Hotline, answering phoned-in questions about stain removal. Call (215) 951-2757, from 9:00 A.M. to 4:00 P.M. Eastern Standard Time, Monday–Friday.

Formerly a Project Engineer at Milliken & Co., Professor Barndt is a member of the American Society for Testing and Materials, the American Association of Textile Chemists and Colorists, the Textured Yarn Association of America and the Association of the Nonwoven Fabrics Industry. He has served as the task group chairman of the Committee on Breaking Load and Elongation for the American Society for Testing and Materials and is a member of the Standards Test Methods Technical Committee for the Association of the Nonwoven Fabrics Industry. For more than ten years, he has made numerous radio and television appearances to promote proper consumer care of textiles.

Professor Barndt was born in 1940. He is married and has three children.